Nan Liu

Sexual Politics in "As You Like It" from Shakespeare

GRIN Verlag

Bibliografische Information der Deutschen Nationalbibliothek:

Die Deutsche Bibliothek verzeichnet diese Publikation in der Deutschen National-
bibliografie; detaillierte bibliografische Daten sind im Internet über http://dnb.d-
nb.de/ abrufbar.

Imprint:

Copyright © 2013 GRIN Verlag GmbH
Druck und Bindung: Books on Demand GmbH, Norderstedt Germany
ISBN: 978-3-656-77059-6

This book at GRIN:

http://www.grin.com/en/e-book/282275/sexual-politics-in-as-you-like-it-from-shake-
speare

GRIN - Your knowledge has value

Der GRIN Verlag publiziert seit 1998 wissenschaftliche Arbeiten von Studenten, Hochschullehrern und anderen Akademikern als eBook und gedrucktes Buch. Die Verlagswebsite www.grin.com ist die ideale Plattform zur Veröffentlichung von Hausarbeiten, Abschlussarbeiten, wissenschaftlichen Aufsätzen, Dissertationen und Fachbüchern.

Visit us on the internet:

http://www.grin.com/

http://www.facebook.com/grincom

http://www.twitter.com/grin_com

1

Contents

1. Introduction

As You Like It is "a vital exploration of gender, the male and the female within us all" (Gay 76). And Arden is "a realm where you can dress up and change your gender, change your way of life" (*ibid.*). I agree with this statement. But before my analysis, I want to elaborate on the relationship between sex and gender identity. Sex is determined by nature, whereas gender is a cultural construct which is influenced by power, ideology, class and ethnicity. To put it differently, women are not confined to be compassionate and submissive and men to be active and dominant just due to their biological differences. However, people in the 16th century were restricted to their traditional gender roles. For example, women were 'The Angel in the House' and men exerted control over 'the weaker vessel', which refers to women because of Christian traditions and allegedly scientific reasons.

In *As You Like It*, we will find out the transcendence of restricted gender roles. To prove my thesis, I will first explore Rosalind's female role playing and male role playing by virtue of the costume. Then Orlando's acquisition of traditionally labeled feminine attributes is to be analyzed. In the last part of my essay, I will come to a conclusion about sexual politics in *As You Like It*.

2. Rosalind's Expansion of Sexual Identity

In order to avoid "the normal vulnerability to male force" (Erickson 22), Rosalind decides to disguise herself as a male. Even if she achieves masculine strength through arming herself with a 'curtal-axe' and 'boar-spear', Rosalind still realizes her inner weakness: "Lie there what hidden woman's fear there will" (Shakespeare 123). She could not overcome the restrictions of her inner feminine self.

After entering the forest of Arden, Rosalind comes across one poem, which reflects deep love towards her. And then she begs Celia "with most petitionary vehemence, tell me who it is" (*ibid.* 164). She confides to Celia that she is still a woman at her core: "Good my complexion! Dost thou think, though I am caparisoned like a man, I have a doublet and hose in my disposition?" (*ibid.* 164-65) She keeps asking about Orlando's situation and interrupts her 'coz'. Her inconstancy of mind and tendency to be disquieted expose her interior (femininity): "Do you not know I am a woman? When I think, I must speak" (*ibid.* 167). In comparison with males' "prescribed 'correct' methods of organization, rationalist rules of logic, and linear reasoning" (Tyson 101), Rosalind's freely associative thinking shadows her disguised male image with femininity.

Under the disguise of the male costume, Rosalind takes the initiative to have access to Orlando and controls him. She seemingly teaches Orlando how to 'woo' her, but in the process she paves the way to be a submissive wife. It is on their first date that Orlando comes late. "But why did he swear he would come this morning, and comes not?" (Shakespeare 179) She cannot control herself and gives away her weak affections: "Never talk to me. I will weep" (*ibid.* 178). Celia instantly points out, "but yet have the grace to consider that tears do not become a man" (*ibid.*). Even though Rosalind plays a male role, she remains an emotional woman.

In Rosalind's response to Phoebe and Silvius, she ostensibly uses her wit to manipulate their relationship but actually criticizes the former's pride and pitilessness and the latter's abasement. For Rosalind, it is only compliant women that can engage in love. She is afraid of following in Phoebe's footsteps. So as to avoid pouring scorn further upon Orlando, e.g. "speak to him like a saucy lackey, and under that habit to play the knave with him" (*ibid*. 168), she determines to be a "busy actor in their play" (*ibid*. 180) and "alerts her to the potential Phoebe in herself" (Erickson 21). What Rosalind endeavors to do is to prepare herself for "voluntary re-entry into the patriarchy" (Gay 48).

Before entering the real marriage, Rosalind asks Celia to be "the priest and marry us" (*ibid*. 191). Through the wedding rehearsal, she wants to educate Orlando how to be a good husband. Although she attempts to vilify herself as a wife who cuckolds her husband, in fact she warns Orlando against disloyalty. The above argument is strongly reinforced by her worry about his departure: "Alas, dear love, I cannot lack thee two hours!" (*ibid*. 194) Facing male's betrayal she is vulnerable: "Ay, go your ways, go your ways; I knew what you would prove" (*ibid*.). She threatens him to keep the promise, or he would be regarded as "the most hollow lover" (*ibid*. 195). As a matter of fact, Rosalind does so out of her fears of being abandoned.

Rosalind's male role begins to break down when she faints at the sight of Orlando's 'bloody napkin'. She can no longer cover her feminine instincts and her debility is fully shown. Therefore Oliver questions disguised Rosalind's masculinity: "You a man? / You lack a man's heart" (*ibid*. 206). As to the explanation of Rosalind's fainting, Hayles puts it, "her faint is a literal relinquishing of conscious control; within the conventions of the play, it is also an involuntary revelation of female gender because fainting is as 'feminine response'" (Hayles 66).

It seems that Rosalind resolves the conflicts between herself and Orlando, Phoebe and Silvius in a flexible and accommodating way. Actually, "Rosalind functions as the fulfiller of desires only as they accord with the laws of patriarchal civilization" (Green 45). "(To Orlando) I will satisfy you if ever I satisfy man, and you shall be married tomorrow" (Shakespeare 214). The line implies that Rosalind is the object of male desire. Influenced by the patriarchal norms and values, she regards the subjection to man's will as the social order. She prepares herself for satisfying him. "(To Silvius) I will content you if what pleases you contents you, and you shall be married tomorrow" (*ibid*.). Due to Silvius' pursuit of heterosexual love and his male identity, Rosalind makes effort to 'content' him, or to put in another way, to cater to patriarchy. By comparison, Phoebe's homosexual thoughts are totally countered. "I will marry you if ever I marry woman, and I'll be married tomorrow" (*ibid.*). In early modern England, female sexuality was unacceptable because of the patriarchal structure.

In the final scene, we will find that Rosalind is a typical patriarchal woman. The *deus ex machina* – Hymen, the god of marriage and the embodiment of chastity, not only performs marriage ceremonies for four heterosexual couples but also reminds Rosalind of "the most goodly treasure that a woman can have" (Vives 165). In the society dominated by males, besides dowry, women's chastity also attracts men's attention. This attraction has been present in Orlando's quest for Rosalind. For example, fantasy of her 'chaste eye' is clearly expressed in his love poem.

Other than chastity, women's subjection is also the product of patriarchal society. Rosalind declares to her father and Orlando: "To you I give myself, for I am yours" (Shakespeare 223). Her unique identity is Other, whereas males are the Subject and the Absolute. As to otherness, De Beauvoir explained that it is "a fundamental category of human thought", which means that "The subject can be posed only in being opposed – he sets himself up as the essential as opposed to the other, the inessential, the object" (17). She voluntarily confines herself to the traditional roles of daughter and wife. In other words, she is already assimilated by patriarchal civilization. "If there be truth in sight, you are my daughter" (Shakespeare 223). To Duke Senior, Rosalind is his daughter unchangeably. She must obey him because the father is the basis of society. However, to Orlando, "If there be truth in sight, you are my Rosalind" (*ibid.*). He hints at her subjection to male hegemony. 'My Rosalind' is supposed to be involved in the feminine sphere – taking care of the household, bearing and nurturing. In the patriarchal society, to be submissive to the husband is the gender ideal of women. She transfers herself from being controlled by father to husband, which means that she falls into oblivion in marriage.

3. Orlando's Femininity

Orlando plays the traditional female role of nurturance when he seeks food for Adam who is dying of hunger. "If I bring thee not something to eat, I will give thee leave to die" (*ibid.* 142). At the risk of 'savage' assaults he still tries to be Adam's 'foster-nurse'. 'With sword drawn', he threatens Duke Senior and his followers in order to save his 'good old man'. However, they are not as 'savage' as Orlando images. Therefore, he exudes tenderness: "If ever from your eyelids wiped a tear, / And know what 'tis to pity, and be pitied, / Let gentleness my strong enforcement be. / In the which hope I blush, and hide my sword" (*ibid.* 149). Due to his 'gentleness', he is welcomed and aided by the "benevolent patriarchy" (Erickson 32). At the same time, his maternal love and nurturing capacity is manifested incisively and vividly: "Whiles, like a doe, I go to find my fawn" (Shakespeare 150).

Traces of Orlando's submissiveness to Rosalind can be found in Act 1: "O poor Orlando! Thou art overthrown / Or Charles, or something weaker, masters thee" (*ibid.* 116). Although he has won the powerful Charles through his masculine strength, he could not conquer Rosalind but is conquered by her. He indoctrinates himself with the idea that he should obey and follow her instructions. His subservience strikes against the common values and behavior standards of the male society which advocates the dominant role of men. As Aughterson said, "He ought to be the leader and auctor of love" (436). If we look at Orlando's poems, his Petrarchan love for Rosalind is explicitly expressed. "Thus Rosalind of many parts / By heavenly synod was devis'd / Of many faces, eyes, and hearts, / To have the touches dearest priz'd. / Heaven would that she these gifts should have, / And I to live and die her slave" (Shakespeare 162-63). The more he idealizes Rosalind, the more subordinate he feels to her. She is so perfect that Orlando dares not approach her. He is willing to be 'her slave' all his life. Female domination strongly contrasts with male humility.

Last but not least, I want to mention Orlando's compassion. In order to rescue his brother from the lioness, Orlando disregards his own safety. "Twice did he turn his back, and purposed so. / But kindness, noble ever than revenge, / And nature, stronger than his just occasion, / Made him give battle to the lioness" (*ibid.* 204). Even if his brother treats him in a ruthless way, such as deprives him of 'good education' and even plans to burn his lodging, Orlando still shows the compassionate part of his masculine nature. But in Renaissance England kindness and mercy are associated with femininity, that is, they are the traditional attributes only to label females.

4. Conclusion

Gender is a cultural construct. Natural sexuality cannot determine one's gender. A male can be either masculine or feminine, so can a female. In the Epilogue, we know that Rosalind is played by a boy. Playing a role within a role, the boy actor explores the unknown field – the realm of the feminine. Because the sexual boundaries are so clear cut that Orlando and Duke Senior cannot recognize Rosalind. Though the traditional gender roles make distinctions between the narrow femininity and masculinity, disguised Rosalind successfully surpasses these boundaries by virtue of the male costume. Orlando places femininity such as maternal nurturance, submissiveness and compassion upon himself. He also challenges the gender hierarchy.

5. Works Cited

Aughterson, Kate, ed. *The English Renaissance. An Anthology of Sources and Documents.* London: Routledge, 1998.

Beauvoir, Simone de. *The Second Sex.* New York: Vintage Books, 1973.

Erickson, Peter. *Patriarchal Structures in Shakespeare's Drama.* Berkeley: University of California Press, 1985.

Gay, Penny. *As She Likes It: Shakespeare's Unruly Women.* London: Routledge, 1994.

Green, Douglas E. "The 'Unexpressive She': Is There Really a Rosalind?" *Journal of Dramatic Theory and Criticism* 2 (1988): 41-52.

Hayles, Nancy K. "Sexual Disguise in 'As You Like It' and 'Twelfth Night'." *Shakespeare Survey: An Annual Survey of Shakespeare Studies and Production* 32 (1979): 63-72.

Shakespeare, William. *The Oxford Shakespeare: As You Like It.* Ed. Alan Brissenden. Oxford: Oxford University Press, 1993.

Tyson, Lois. *Critical Theory Today: A User-Friendly Guide.* London: Routledge, 2006.

Vives, Juan L. "Instruction of a Christian Woman." *Renaissance Woman: A Sourcebook.* Ed. Kate Aughterson. London: Routledge, 1995. 165.